better together*

*This book is best read together, grownup and kid.

 akidsco.com

a
kids
book
about

a kids book about

PHILANTHROPY

by Jeunai Emery

a
kids
book
about

Printed in the United States of America.

A Kids Book About books are available online: *akidsco.com*

To share your stories, ask questions, or inquire about bulk
purchases (schools, libraries, and nonprofits), please use
the following email address: *hello@akidsco.com*

Print ISBN: 978-1-958825-71-6
Ebook ISBN: 978-1-958825-72-3

Designed by Rick DeLucco
Edited by Emma Wolf

To Morfar, whose generosity lit the path.
To Kaelyn and Theo, the bright hearts of tomorrow.
This book is dedicated to the spirit of
giving that connects generations.

Intro

What comes to mind for you when you hear the word "philanthropy"? If you're like most people, you likely think of super wealthy people making multimillion-dollar gifts. At the very least, there is a strong association with donations.

But philanthropy is so much more than that!

I truly believe that we can change the world through authentic, passionate, and effective philanthropy. This means taking action for good in areas that are personally and deeply important to us.

With this book, I hope to offer a simple and accessible definition of a sometimes confusing word. I also hope to help kids and families reflect on what matters to them, encourage each of our unique passions, and empower us all to take action.

Hi! My name is JEUNAI.

It's a tricky name to say, so let me help.

It's pronounced like: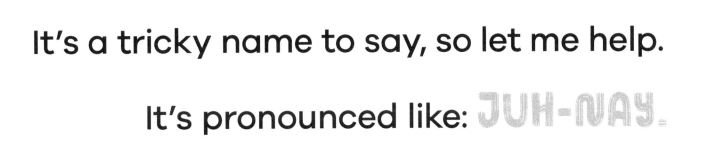

I want to talk to you about another word that can be difficult to say: philanthropy.

Let's all say it together:

THRO-PY.

NICE JOB!

Have you heard this word before?

Do you know what it means?

WELL...

Have you ever visited a museum?

Has your family ever picked up food at a food bank?

Have you or someone you know ever participated in a school, club, or team fundraiser?

ALL THESE THINGS ARE POSSIBLE BECAUSE OF PHILANTHROPY!

People in this kind of work usually define philanthropy as...

VOLUNTARY ACTION FOR THE PUBLIC GOOD.

Let's break down what that means!

"VOLUNTARY ACTION"

means doing things because you want to, not because you have to.

The 3 main examples of voluntary action are:

1. **VOLUNTEERING,** which is when you use your time and energy to help others. This can look like spending time with animals at your local shelter or picking up trash in your neighborhood.

2. **DONATING,** which is when you give money or things to help others. This can include giving clothes to an organization which can distribute them to people in need.

3. **ADVOCACY,** which means bringing attention to a cause or a problem in order to help find a solution.

For example, my grandpa was a pastor who spent a lot of his life advocating for houseless people in his community.

He spent time with people to remind them that they matter, and he even cofounded a nonprofit* organization to offer further support.

*A nonprofit is a group of people who work together and instead of making money for themselves, they use the money (or profit) to do good. Sometimes, people call this a charity.

So, we've covered what "voluntary action" is.

How about that "PUBLIC GOOD" part?

"PUBLIC" means something for the community; it's outward-facing.

Doing chores to help your grownups isn't a public good, but picking weeds in your community garden is!

Now, everyone has different perspectives on what is "GOOD."

Doing something for the good of others means doing something with the intent of bettering the world.

HOW WOULD YOU LIKE
TO CHANGE THE WORLD?

IS THERE SOMETHING
YOU WISH WAS
DIFFERENT, OR BETTER?

WHAT MAKES
YOU HAPPY?

HOW COULD YOU USE
THAT HAPPINESS TO
HELP OTHERS?

These kinds of questions inspire philanthropy everywhere.

Maybe it seems like the things you care about are too big for someone your age.

But the truth is,
philanthropy is for

EVERYONE.

And kids like you can (and do)
make a difference every day!

SO, WHERE D

O WE START?

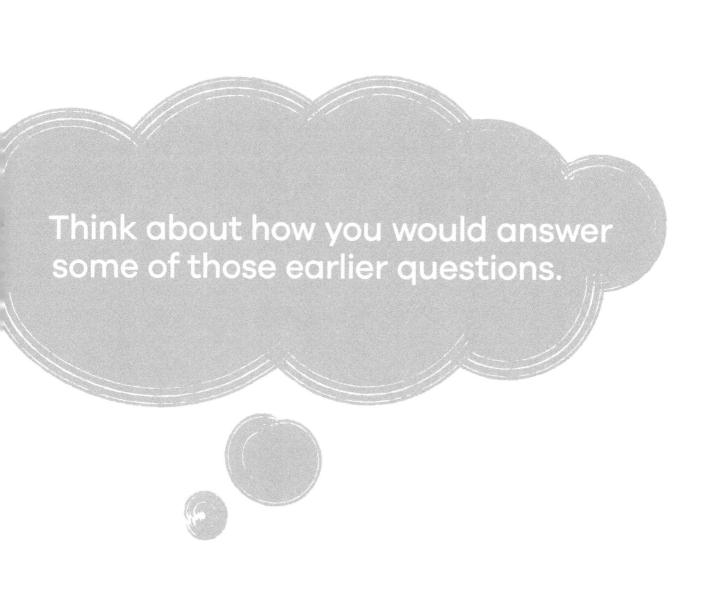

Think about how you would answer some of those earlier questions.

Also, think about some things you're really good at or like to do.

THEN...

COMBINE

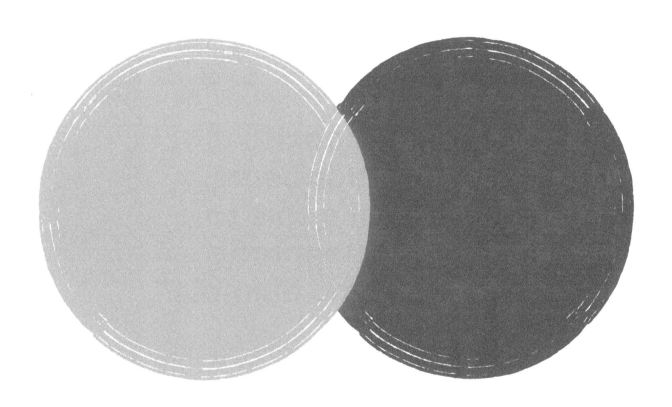

THEM!

If you love baking cookies and care about polar bears, you can have a bake sale to raise money for a nonprofit which protects arctic animals.

If you love hiking and care about the environment, you can organize a group hike to clean up the trails in your community.

If you love writing and care about current events, you can talk to your teacher about starting a newsletter so your classmates can learn more about current events.

For me, one thing I really care about is kids (yes, that means you, too!).

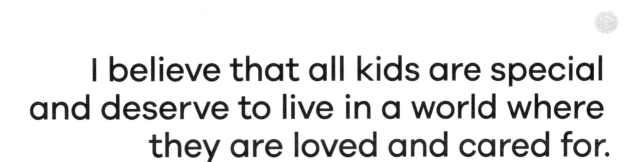

I believe that all kids are special and deserve to live in a world where they are loved and cared for.

When I volunteer, donate, or advocate, I look for opportunities that help kids.

FOR EXAMPLE, one year for my birthday, instead of gifts, I asked my friends and family to send diapers as a donation to a nonprofit which collects baby items to provide for families in need.

My friends and family also helped me make this book, because talking about philanthropy with kids is really important!

AND, DO YOU KNOW WHY?

Because kids are really good at

ING BIG.

And we need big dreams to
make the world a better place.

What you care about is

IMPORTANT.

There is no idea too big
or action too small to
make a difference.

And your dreams of what the world could be can make a...

HUGE IMPACT.

Hold onto what you care about and let it motivate you to take action to create the world you want to see.

YOU CAN
START
TODAY!

Outro

Now that we've reached the end of the book, what comes to mind when you think of the word "philanthropy"? Understanding philanthropy as voluntary action for the public good can open up a world of possibilities for everyone alike. (Shout-out to Robert L. Payton and Michael P. Moody for the awesome definition!)

Inspired by what you and the kids in your life care about, like to do, or are good at, I hope you know that you can make a big impact on the world around you!

Still need some inspiration on how to get started? Visit **charitynavigator.com** to search nonprofit organizations by cause, location, and more. From there, you can select a charity to support by volunteering, donating, or advocating.

You can make a difference, and you can start today!

About The Author

Jeunai Emery (she/her) wrote this book for any kid who wants to make an impact. Fueled by the belief that kids have important ideas and the drive to effect change, she emphasizes the crucial role grownups play in recognizing and nurturing these passions. Speaking from over a decade of experience in the advancement of higher education and the nonprofit sector, she simplifies what it means to give back in real and impactful ways.

Inspired by her 2 kids, Jeunai is dedicated to fostering a generation of compassionate change makers. She is on a mission to equip families and kids who are eager to dive into the world of philanthropy. Her journey is marked by a commitment to amplifying young voices and creating a brighter tomorrow.

 @kids.philanthropy.project   @KidsPhilanthropyProject

 kidsphilanthropyproject.com

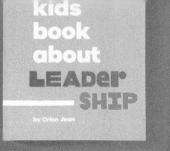

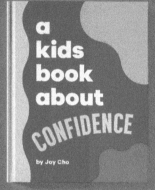

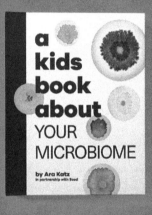

Printed in the USA
CPSIA information can be obtained
at www.ICGtesting.com
LVHW060316160224
771975LV00012B/223